CRAFTY IDEAS WITH PAINTING

Melanie Rice

Illustrated by Lynne Farmer

Photography by Chris Fairclough

HODDER AND STOUGHTON
LONDON SYDNEY AUCKLAND TORONTO

To Chris, Catherine and Alex, for all their help.

British Library Cataloguing in Publication Data

Rice, Melanie
   Crafty ideas with painting.
   1. Activities using paints
   I. Title   II. Farmer, Lynne   III. Fairclough, Chris
   751.4

   ISBN 0-340-52572-X

Text copyright © Melanie Rice 1991
Illustrations copyright © Lynne Farmer 1991

First published 1991

All rights reserved. No part of this publication may be reproduced or transmitted in any form or by any means, electronically or mechanically, including photocopying, recording, or any information storage and retrieval system, without either prior permission in writing from the publisher or a licence permitting restricted copying. In the United Kingdom such licences are issued by the Copyright Licensing Agency, 33-34 Alfred Place, London WC1E 7DP.

The rights of Melanie Rice to be identified as the author of the text of this work and of Lynne Farmer to be identified as the illustrator of this work have been asserted by them in accordance with the Copyright, Designs and Patents Act 1988.

Published by Hodder and Stoughton Children's Books, a division of Hodder and Stoughton Ltd, Mill Road, Dunton Green, Sevenoaks, Kent TN13 2YA

Design by Sally Boothroyd

Cover illustration by Lynn Breeze

Book list compiled by Peter Bone, Senior Librarian, Children's and Schools Services, Hampshire County Library

Printed in Great Britain by BPCC Hazell Books
Paulton, Bristol
Member of BPCC Ltd

CONTENTS

	Page
Notes to readers	4
Bottle bookends	6
Fish mobile	8
Glass prints	10
Face painting	12
Spray painting	14
Beautiful brushes	16
Gift boxes	18
Two-way picture	20
Buried treasure game	22
Shiny wax painting	24
Rainbow candles	26
Badges	28
Book list	30
Index	31

Note to parents and teachers

All the ideas in this book can easily be carried out at home or at school. Every item has been made by my own young children and then photographed for this book. Each page has clear instructions accompanied by numbered, easy-to-follow illustrations.

A variety of surfaces has been used for the activities: card, glass, paper and so on.

We used powder and poster paints, both of which can be mixed to obtain various thicknesses and textures. Watercolour blocks are a cheap and economical alternative but they do not produce such strong colours.

Finding somewhere to leave finished paintings to dry can be a problem. It's best to put them on something which they will not stick to, such as a piece of plastic or wax paper, but newspaper will do. Some can be hung up on a washing line!

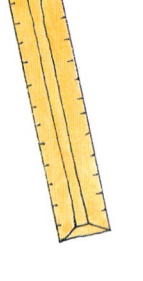

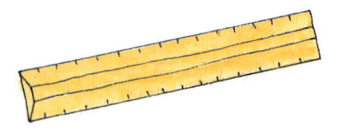

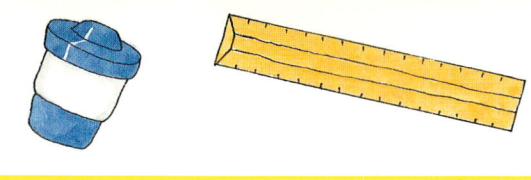

Note to children

Things to remember:

1. Read all instructions carefully before you begin so that you know what you have to do. Use the illustrations to help you.

2. Make sure everything you need is ready before you start.

3. Spread newspaper over your working surface – this is especially important for messy projects.

4. Clean up any mess when you have finished.

5. Put everything away tidily.

At the end of each project I have suggested more things for you to make. Maybe you have some ideas of your own. Don't be afraid to try them out.

Melanie Rice

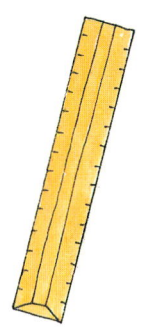

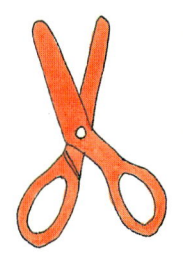

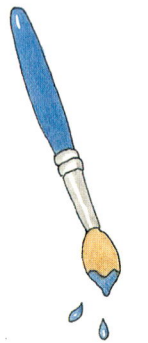

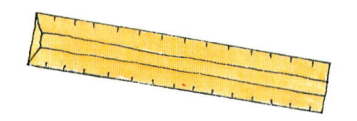

BOTTLE BOOKENDS

These cheerful characters will help keep your books from falling over.

You will need:

2 empty bottles
cardboard
egg cup
glue
paintbrush and white spirit
paper
poster or watercolour paint and paintbrush
small stones or sand
2 table tennis balls
white emulsion paint
wool

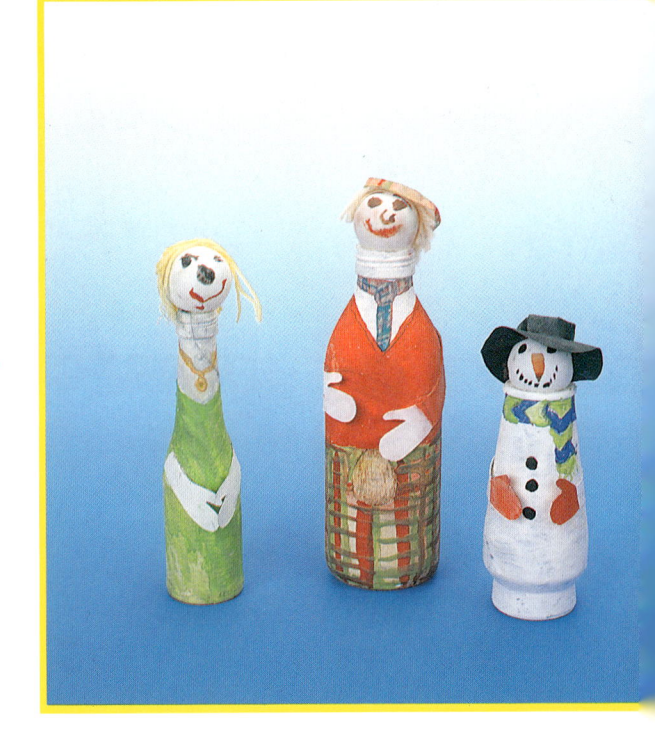

1. Paint both bottles with white emulsion paint and leave to dry. (Keep some white spirit nearby to clean your fingers and brushes.)

2. Fill the bottles with small stones or sand.

3. Stick a table tennis ball over the top of each bottle.

4. Cut out cardboard arms and hands and stick to the bottles as shown.

5 Paint faces and clothing and stick on wool as hair.

6 To make a beret: place an egg cup on some paper and draw round the base. Cut out the circle and make small cuts round the edge. Fold up the edge and secure with a strip of paper.

7 To make a snowman's hat: draw a circle on a piece of paper, then draw another circle around it. Cut out the inner circle as shown. Now cut out a strip of paper (about 2cm wide) and make cuts along both edges. Fold the edges in and out, sticking the circle to the top edge and the ring to the bottom edge, as shown.

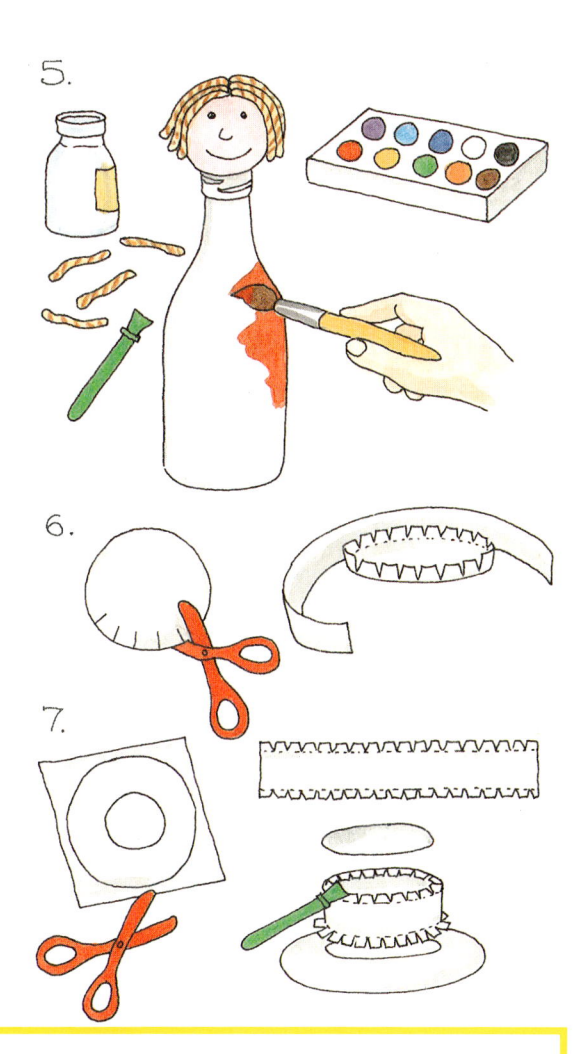

Stones can be painted and decorated in the same way.

You can use them as paperweights to stop your drawings from blowing away.

7

FISH MOBILE

Hang this colourful mobile in front of an open window and it will catch the light as it spins round.

You will need:

cotton thread
blue packaging paper or tissue
glue
paintbrush
pliers
2-ply kitchen paper
poster paints
scissors
sponge
a stick or cane
wire

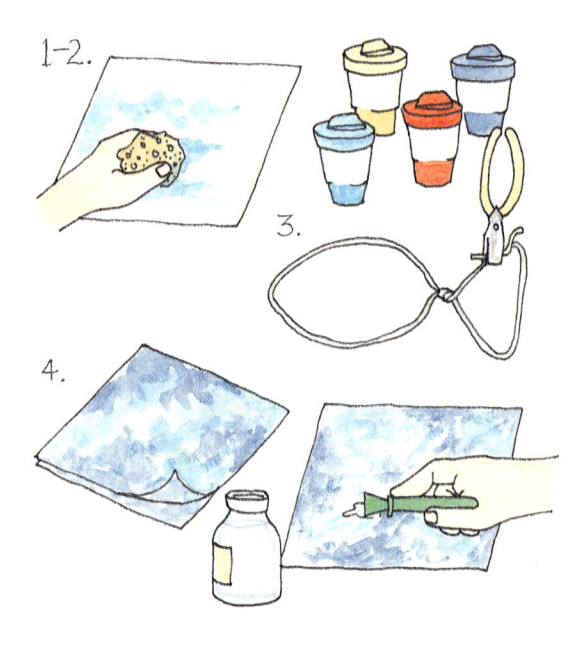

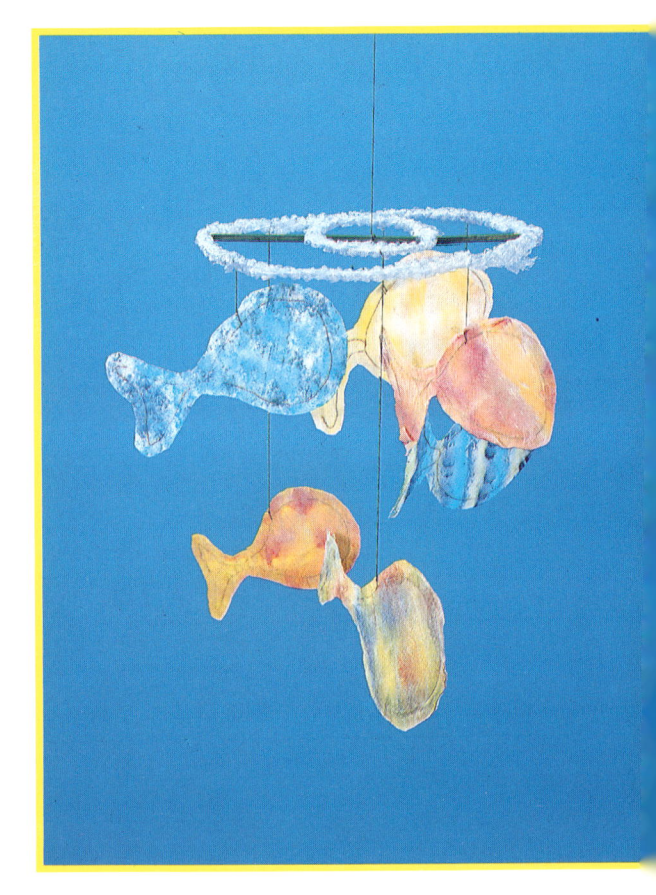

1. Dampen a piece of kitchen paper with a wet sponge, then carefully dab on poster paint.

2. Hang up to dry.

3. Bend a piece of wire into the shape of a fish. (Use pliers to twist the two ends together.)

4. Carefully pull apart the paper to make two pieces, and spread glue over one piece.

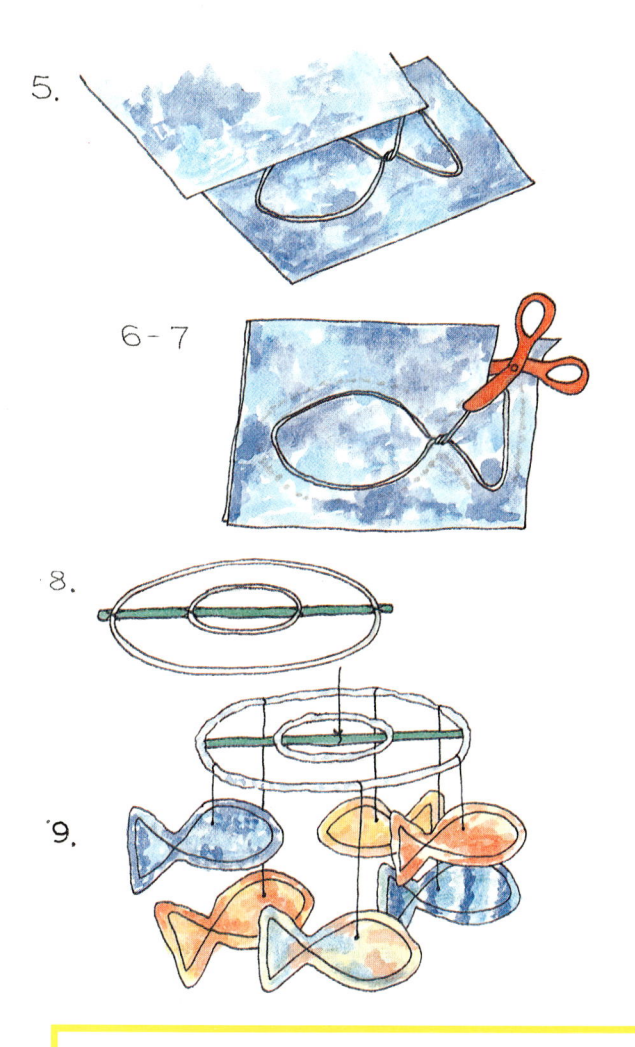

5 Place the wire fish on to the glue, then stick the second piece of paper on top. Leave to dry.

6 Cut round the shape of the fish about 1cm from the wire.

7 Then make five more fish in the same way.

8 Make two circles of wire and bind them to the stick as shown. Hang the fish from the wire with the cotton thread.

9 Wind blue tissue paper or plastic bubbly packaging material around the wire. Small pieces of Plasticine can be hidden in the tissue to help balance the mobile.

Make a stained glass window.

Cut a frame from black paper or card and stick on kitchen tissue, coloured in the same way as above. To get the best effect, hold up to the light or stick to a window.

GLASS PRINTS

Make an attractive box for your paints and brushes using these eye-catching glass prints.

You will need:

empty cardboard box
  (e.g. a shoe box)
kitchen paper
paintbrush, cardboard comb
  or other paint spreader
poster paints
sheet of glass or plastic
sheet of paper

1 Splodge the paint thickly on to the glass or plastic using a large paintbrush.

2 Spread the paint with your fingers, with paintbrushes or with pieces of cardboard.
(If necessary, wipe some paint away with a piece of kitchen tissue.)

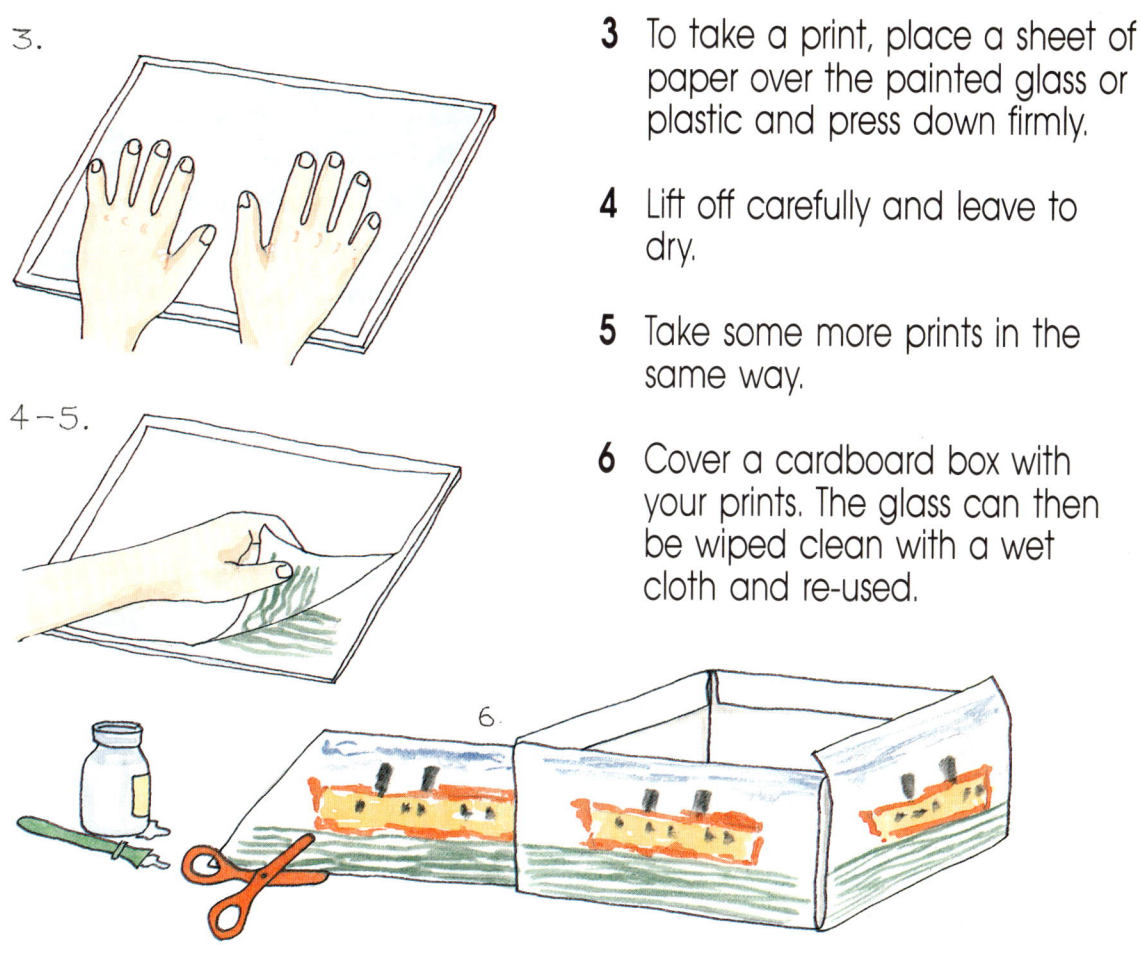

3 To take a print, place a sheet of paper over the painted glass or plastic and press down firmly.

4 Lift off carefully and leave to dry.

5 Take some more prints in the same way.

6 Cover a cardboard box with your prints. The glass can then be wiped clean with a wet cloth and re-used.

Use a wax crayon to draw a picture on the glass, and then spread paint thickly over the top. Take a print.

FACE PAINTING

All over the world, people paint their bodies for decoration – some to look attractive, others for special occasions like fairs, carnivals or ceremonies. This recipe tells you how to make face paints for you and your friends.

You will need:

cheese grater
cooker
25g cornflour
mixing bowl
thin paintbrush
non-toxic powder paints
saucepan
sieve
half a 125g bar of soap
spoon
250ml water
3 yoghurt pots

CAUTION: boiling water can scald. Ask an adult to help.

1 Mix the cornflour with a little water to make a smooth paste.

2 Pour the rest of the water into a saucepan and stir in the paste. Bring to the boil, stirring well, then remove from the heat.

3 Grate the soap into flakes.

4 Drop them into the hot water, a few at a time, and stir until they dissolve.

5 Pour the mixture through a sieve and leave to cool.

6 Divide the mixture between the yoghurt pots, add a teaspoon of different coloured powder paint to each, and mix well.

7 Paint some of the simple designs shown here, using a thin paintbrush.

The paints will wash off easily, but keep some tissues handy in case you make a mistake.

Mehndi

Henna powder, mixed into a paste with lemon juice and drops of warm water, is used in Pakistan and India to decorate the palms of the hands. You can try this but, be warned, the colour lasts for a week.

Alternatively, you could try out some patterns on a cardboard cut-out of your hand.

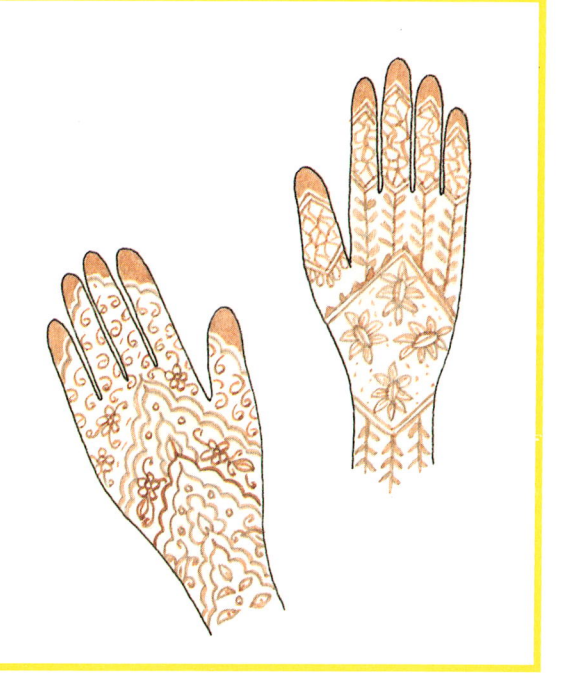

SPRAY PAINTING

Spray paintings are messy to do, but make very effective pictures.

You will need:

card
old knife
paper
poster paints
scissors
old toothbrush

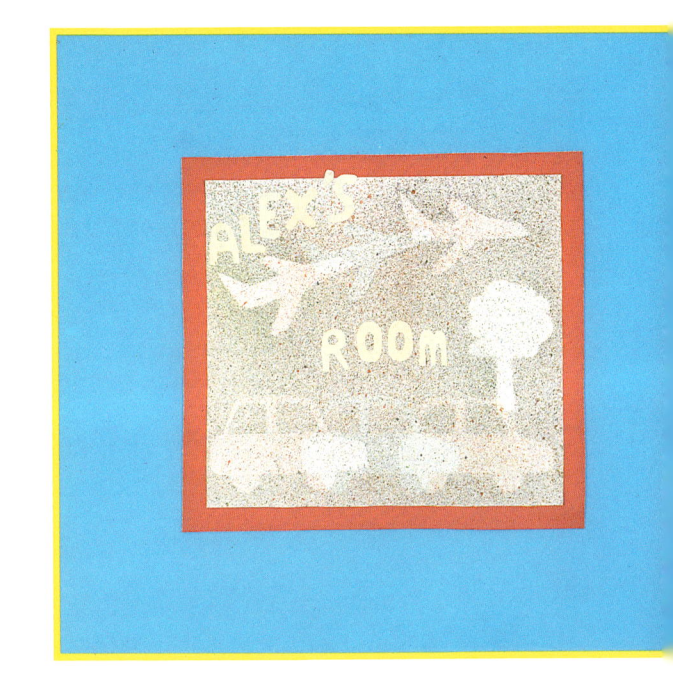

1.

1 Cut some stencils from card. Include shapes of things that move, e.g. people, animals and vehicles.

2 Lay the shapes on a piece of paper.

2.

3 Mix some paint with a little water so that it is quite runny.

4 Dip the toothbrush in the paint, then hold it over the paper with the bristles uppermost.

5 Scrape the blade of the knife across the brush towards you so that paint sprays across the paper.

6 When the paint is dry, move the stencils to a new position and spray with another colour. Repeat until the picture is finished.

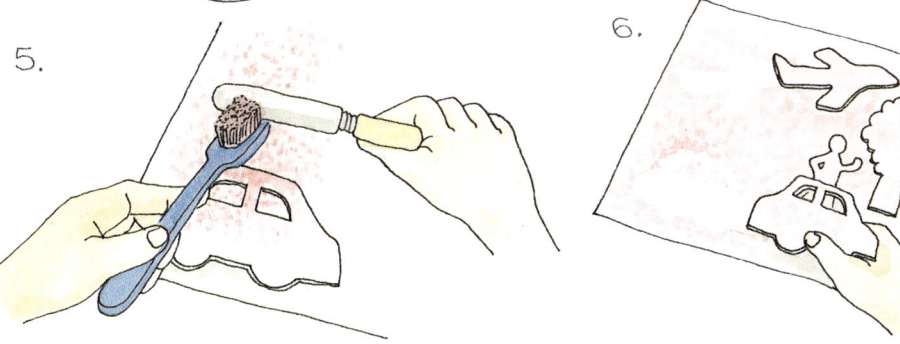

3-4.

5.

6.

Make a poster for your bedroom door. Draw and cut out the letters of your name and the letters of the word ROOM to stick on the picture.

15

BEAUTIFUL BRUSHES

People living in the Pacific Islands enjoy carving and decorating tools and everyday objects found around the home. You can paint similar designs yourself.

You will need:

paintbrush
poster paints
sandpaper
varnish
wooden-handled brush

Here are some of the patterns used by the Islanders. They are called Oceanian patterns.

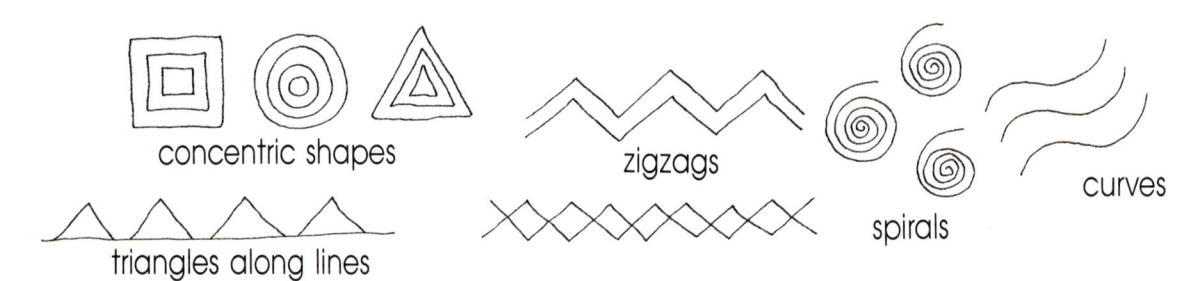

concentric shapes

zigzags

spirals

curves

triangles along lines

1 Rub the wooden top of a brush with sandpaper.

2 Select three or four poster paints and a very fine brush.

16

3.

3 Paint the wood of your brush. Arrange the Oceanian patterns to make your own designs, like the one shown here.

4 Leave to dry.

5 You can make your brush waterproof by painting a layer of varnish over the wood. Leave to dry.

4-5.

Other wooden items can be decorated, too.

Hang this up as a wall decoration.

GIFT BOXES

Home-made gift boxes will make the presents you give your friends and family extra special.

You will need:

2 sheets of card
 (each 420mm × 297mm)
poster or powder paints
pencil and ruler
scissors
string

1.

1 Cut three pieces of string, each about 30cm long.

2 Dip each piece into a different-coloured pot of paint, then lay carefully on a sheet of card, allowing one end of each to hang over the edge.

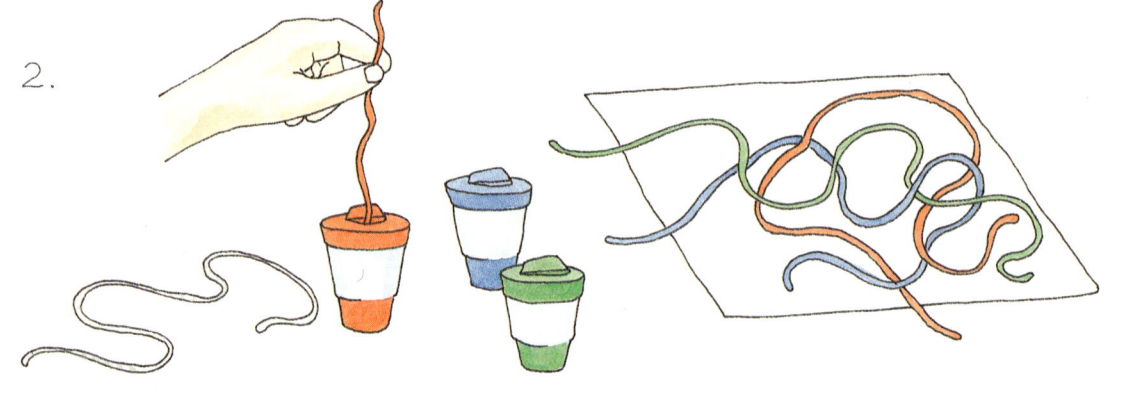

2.

3 Place the second sheet of card on top.

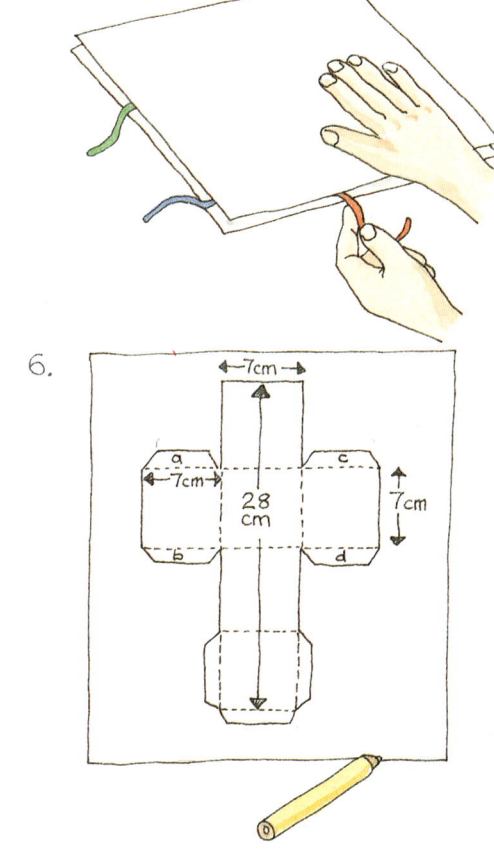

4 Holding the top card firmly in place, slowly pull out each piece of string so that the paint smudges.

5 Carefully separate the two pieces of card and leave to dry.

6 Draw six squares and 'flaps' as shown, on the back of the cards.

7 Cut along the solid lines _____
Fold along the dotted lines........

8 Stick the flaps (a b c d) to the sides to make the boxes.

You can use other things besides brushes for painting. Try some of these –

- string
- a piece of card
- a sponge
- an old comb
- a feather

TWO-WAY PICTURE

Surprise visitors with this picture which will appear to change as they move round the room.

You will need:

2 sheets of card
paintbrush
poster paints
scissors
sticky tape

1 Paint a winter scene on one sheet of card – with snow, bare trees, people wrapped in warm clothes, a frozen pond etc.

2.

1.

2 On the other sheet of card, paint a similar scene in summer – with flowers, leafy trees, people in light clothing etc.

20

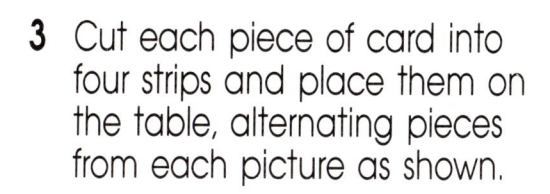

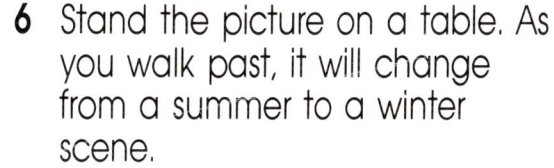

3 Cut each piece of card into four strips and place them on the table, alternating pieces from each picture as shown.

4 Use sticky tape to join the eight pieces together.

5 Pleat the card, fan-like, along the joins.

6 Stand the picture on a table. As you walk past, it will change from a summer to a winter scene.

Another surprise picture

Fold a piece of thin paper in half. On the front draw someone running away.

On the inside, draw the monster he is running away from.

Hold the paper up to the light and you will see the monster chasing the boy.

BURIED TREASURE GAME

Inventing an island of your own can be fun. Show this one to your friends and ask them to help you find the buried treasure.

You will need:

baking tray
cocktail sticks
paper
pencil
poster paints
sand
scissors
sticky tape
sweet

1 Cut out a piece of paper to fit the top of the baking tray. Draw the outline of an island on the paper.

2 Paint picture symbols on the map to show where things are.

volcano
hills and mountains
rocks
cave
wood
swamp
whale
sharks
pirate bones
old landing stage
compass
lake and river
deserted hut

3 Fill the tin with sand and press a wrapped sweet into it.

4 Tape the four corners of the map over the tin.

5 Cut six paper flags and thread the cocktail sticks through them.

6 Ask your family and friends to write their names on the flags and to stick them into the map where they think the treasure is buried.

7 Carefully untape the map and lift up to see whose cocktail stick is nearest the sweet.

You can use sand to make a painting with an interesting texture.

Spread glue over some paper. Pour sand over the glue.

When the glue is dry, shake off the extra sand and paint a picture.

SHINY WAX PAINTING

In the past, manuscript painters used to cover their pictures with tiny patterns – on clothes, building, furniture, and even on the leaves of trees. Using wax crayons and paint, you too can make a picture which is full of patterns.

You will need:

black felt pen
paintbrush
paper
pencil
watercolour paint
wax crayons

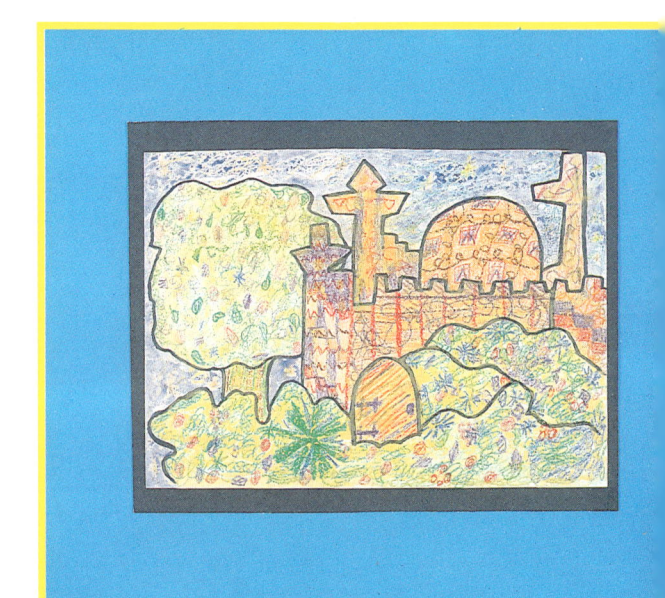

1 Plan your picture in pencil first.

2 Draw round the outlines with a thick black felt pen.

24

3.

3 Fill in as many details as you can, using wax crayons.

4 These are some of the patterns we used.

5 Mix your paint with a little water so that it is quite runny, then paint over the wax patterns, filling the page with colour.

4.

5.

Make a magic picture

Draw a picture using a wax candle.

Give it to a friend to paint over with thin paint until your picture appears.

25

RAINBOW CANDLES

Marbling designs have little veins of colour running through them like real marble. These candles make ideal party decorations.

You will need:

candles
emulsion paints
  (pale and bright colours)
glue
newspaper
paintbrush
plastic cups
scissors
stick
string
bucket of water
white spirit

CAUTION: be careful not to drip paint on anything. Work outside if you can, and prepare a place for the candles to dry before you begin.

1 Paint each plastic cup with a pale emulsion paint and leave to dry.

2 Fill a bucket with water.

3 Drop a blob of paint into the water with a stick. if it does not spread out, add a little white spirit.

4 Drop in some more colours and swirl the water round.

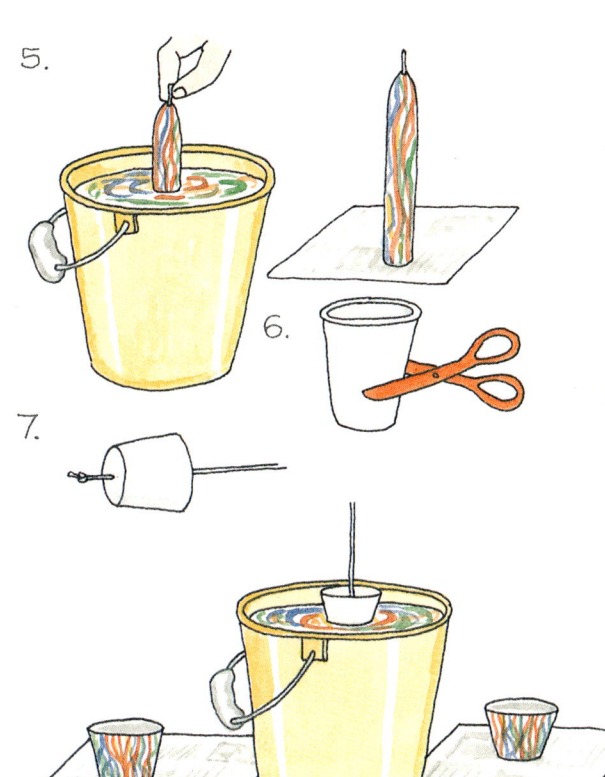

5 Hold each candle by its wick, dip it into the bucket, then slowly lift out. Stand the candle on some newspaper to dry.

6 Cut a plastic cup in half.

7 Thread a piece of knotted string through the bottom, then dip into the bucket.

8 When the paint has dried, stick the candle into the cup.

Other things can also be marbled:

cardboard boxes

old canvas shoes

flowerpots

27

BADGES

Make badges for yourself and your friends, using your own special designs.

You will need:

card
fabric paints
an iron
masking tape
material
mug
pencil
scissors
sponge

1 Cut your material into circles. To get the right size draw round a mug.

2 Draw the outline of the design you want on a piece of card. Make sure the design is a little smaller than the circle of material.

3 Cut out carefully to make a stencil.

4.

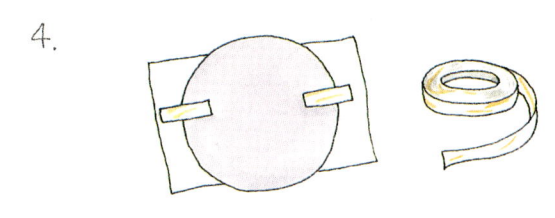

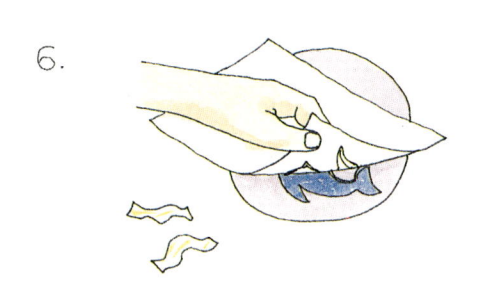

5.

6.

4 Stick the stencil to the material with masking tape.

5 Dab on the paint with a piece of sponge. Fill the shape but be careful not to let paint seep under the card.

6 Remove the stencil and leave the badge to dry.

7 Ask an adult to iron the badge to fix the fabric paint.

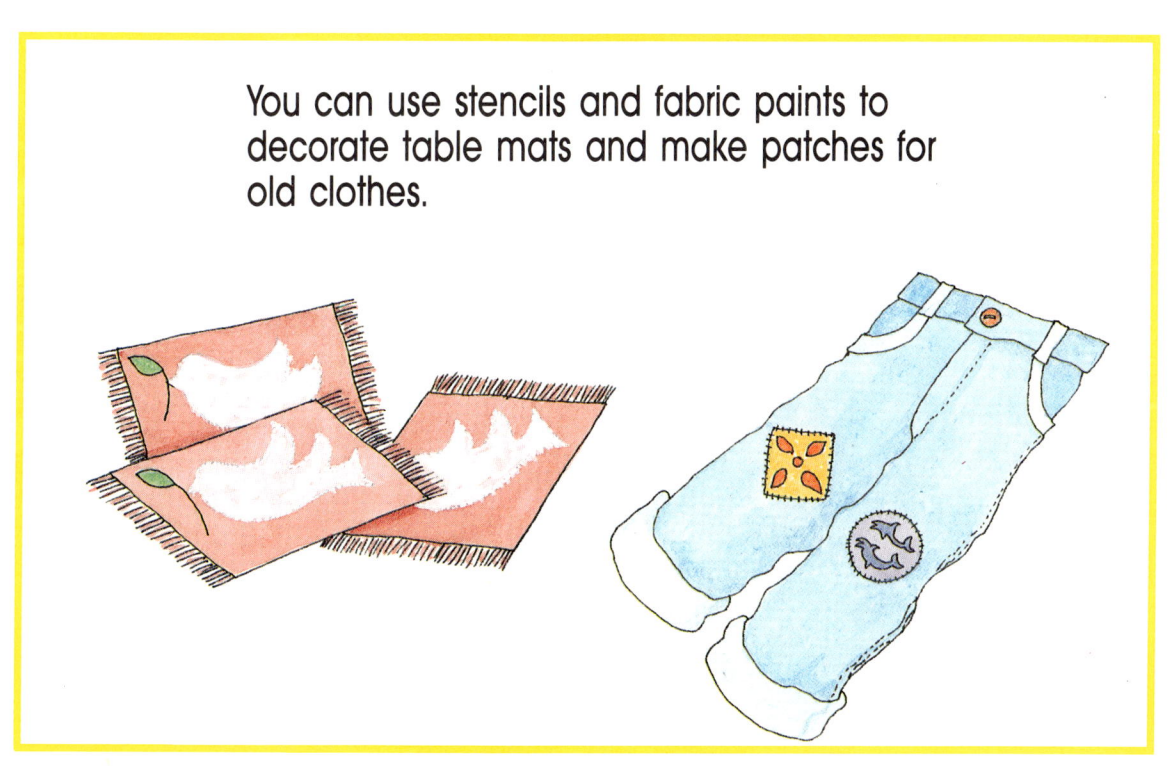

7.

You can use stencils and fabric paints to decorate table mats and make patches for old clothes.

BOOK LIST

For more ideas and more difficult painting projects, the following books will help. Your local library should be able to get copies for you.

Cooke, Jean.
PROJECTS FOR EASTER.
Wayland, 1989. 1852103663
Decorating eggs can be quite a challenge and this book has a description of how it can be done.

Devonshire, Hilary.
DRAWING.
Franklin Watts, 1989. 0863138977
Included in this book are sections on using watercolours and poster paints. Other books in the *Fresh Start* series may help as well, particularly **Collage** and **Printing.**

Foster, Patience.
USBORNE GUIDE TO PAINTING.
Usborne, 1981. 0860205479
Everything you will need to know if you are going to paint more seriously.

Pluckrose, Henry.
PAINTS.
Franklin Watts, 1987. 0863135773
Colourful ideas for using paint with different kinds of materials. Another book in the well illustrated *Fresh Start* series.

INDEX

badges 28-29
bookends 6-7
brushes 16-17

candles 26-27

emulsion paint 6, 26

face paints 12

games 22-23
gift boxes 10-11, 18-19

magic picture 25
marbling 26-27
Mehndi 13
mobiles 8-9
moving picture 21

Oceanic design 16-17

paperweights 7
patches 29
prints 10-11
posters 15
poster paints 6, 8, 10, 14, 20, 22
powder paints 12, 13, 18

sand 22, 23
spray painting 14-15
stained glass window 9
stencils 14, 15, 29

table-mats 29
two-way picture 20-21

watercolour paint 6, 24
wax painting 24-25